The Fearless Girl and The Little Guy with Greatness

Live Life Motivated

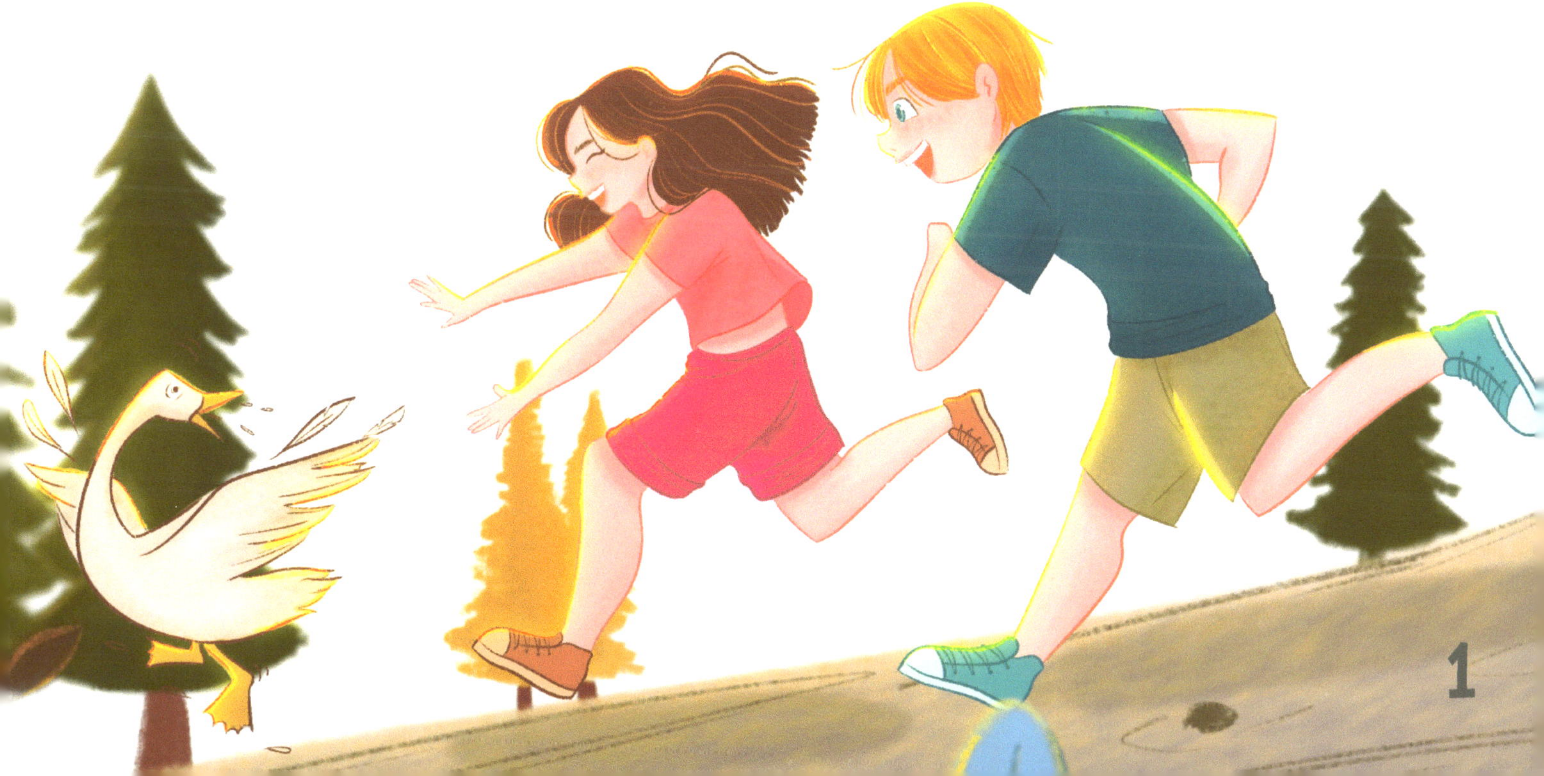

Written by
Mort Greenberg &
Carly Greenberg

Copyright © 2023 by
Mort Greenberg & Carly Greenberg

Design: Heri Susanto
Illustrations: Dian Kartika Abidin

First Paperback edition February 2023

ISBN 979-8-9873618-0-1

Published by TuckEmIn
www.tuckemin.com

Introduction

Tuck Em' In Publishing is a father and daughter effort that creates and publishes books for kids. Our mission is to Motivate and Inspire. Our vision is to help kids make the most of their todays and tomorrows.

The Fearless Girl and The Little Guy with Greatness is a book series that aims to share the following message: anything is possible for any kid if they put their mind to it. The format of each page or scenario is to allow for an interactive back-and-forth between parent/guardian and child.

Kids, you can find in our books ways to handle yourselves in important, real-life situations. Caregivers, you will find ways to push your kids to be their best selves. Through our books, we hope to encourage families to communicate more effectively with each other.

This book, titled "Live Life Motivated," is the first installment in our series. There are four sections to this book: 1) Making The Most of Your Day, 2) Interacting with Other People, 3) Becoming the Best You Can Be, and 4) Growing Up & Going to Work.

Each scenario has four parts to it: a question, an answer, an explanation, and room to write in/talk through a real-life example. First, the parent/guardian asks the question. After talking about the answer to said question, the caregiver should then offer further explanation for clarity. Finally, the caregiver asks the child to give an example in their own words.

Mort Greenberg and his daughter, Carly Greenberg, have embarked on numerous adventures together across the mountains of the United States. They also built self-guided, 18-hour day races in London, Paris, Milan, Venice, Murano, Burano, Rome, Buenos Aires, Tigre, Montevideo, Valparaiso, Santiago, Asuncion, and more.

This father and daughter team has worked through and overcome the same situations that you, as a parent, are experiencing now with a young daughter or son. Each scenario in the book was an actual conversation that took place over the years from when Carly was three to ten years old.

You Can Follow **Mort** and **Carly** on social media:

@mortgreenberg

@greenbergcarly

@mortgreenberg

@carlygreenberg

This Book Belongs to

_____

Today's Date : _____

Sections
(Table Of Contents)

Making The Most Of Your Day

Hi there! Welcome to the "Making the Most of Your Day" section! Do you want to learn how to make **each day the best it can be?** Great! We're going to talk about three important things that can help. First, we're going to talk about how anything is possible as long as you tell yourself that "you can do it." Next, we'll talk about how to get better at something. We'll learn about practicing an working hard to improve at things we enjoy. Finally, we'll talk about how life is all about making choices and prioritizing the things we do each and every day.

What Type of Person Are You?

"I'm A Take-Charge Person"

Anything is possible, you just need to tell yourself that you can do it!

Picture in your mind what you want. Then set out to accomplish that.

What do you want to accomplish?

_____

_____

_____

_____

_____

_____

How Do You Get Better at Something?

"Practice, Practice, Practice!"

It takes time to learn new things. You just have to keep trying and trying to get better and better.

Practicing something you enjoy doing will make you very, very good at it. The more you practice, the better you will get!

What do you want to Practice?

_____

_____

_____

_____

_____

_____

13

What Is Life All About?

"Life Is All About Making Choices"

What is important to you? If there are three items you like, but you can only have one, which one are you going to choose?

We cannot have everything. That said, by prioritizing what's most important to us, we are certain to make the right decision and therefore, the right choice.

What choices have you had to make recently?

_____

_____

_____

_____

_____

Interacting with
Other People

Welcome to Section #2 of your book: **Interacting With Other People!** In this section, we will explore how to listen to others, what to do when we need help, and how to solve problems. It is important to remember that we are all different, and that is okay. By learning to listen and work well with others, we can accomplish great things! Are you ready to get started? Let's go!

How Do You Hear Others?

"Listen!"

We always want to be heard and so do our friends. A great friend is someone who listens, and understands when their friends are happy, sad, or need to talk about something.

The more you listen to others, the more they will want to build a friendship with you.

Who have you listened to recently?

_____

_____

_____

_____

_____

_____

What If You Are Not Able To Do Something Alone?

"Ask For Help"

Just as anyone else would when in need of aid, you too should not be afraid to ask for a helping hand.

People like to help. Even better, the more help you get, the easier it is to do what you want.

When is the last time you asked for help?

_____

_____

_____

_____

_____

_____

How Do You Fix A Problem?

"Improvise, Adapt, And Overcome!"

There are no problems – just challenges to overcome. Each challenge is an opportunity to exercise your mind and find a solution to whatever problem you may have.

So, find a new way to do something. Make that new way work for you as well as others. Embrace it!

What problems have you recently fixed?

_____

_____

_____

_____

_____

_____

Become
The Best
You Can Be...

Welcome to Section #3: **Becoming The Best You Can Be**. Here, we're going to talk about four important things. First, we'll talk about forgiving people. Next, we'll talk about the best way to learn about new topics and the power of asking questions. Then, we'll talk about becoming a good friend, and taking care of those who are good to you. Finally, we'll talk about how to make your body feel good through exercise and healthy eating."

Is It OK to Forgive People?

"Always Have Love In Your Heart"

Yes, always forgive. Even if it takes you a little while to do this, always forgive.

You should never hate. Always be willing to forgive people when they do things that you may not like.

Otherwise, it will weigh on your mind, and you will not be able to focus on other things that are important to you.

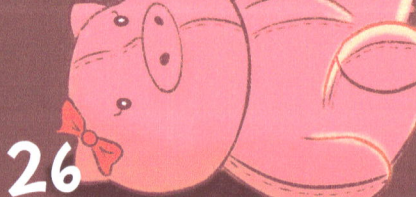

Have you forgiven
anyone lately?

27

What is The Best Way to Learn About New Topics?

"Ask Questions. Lots Of Questions!"

Learning is not just reading, or watching others. Those are both important, but the best way to learn is by asking questions. You can ask questions to yourself and to others!

By asking questions, you will be using your mind to not only think but also understand in new and exciting ways.

What questions did you ask today?

_____

_____

_____

_____

_____

_____

How Do You Become A Good Friend?

"Take Care Of Those Who Are Good To You"

The best friends you will ever have in life are the people who are always good to you. They are good to you every day, every month, and every year.

They do things you like, they say good things to you, and they are there when you want to talk or play. So, in turn, you should also treat them with the same kindness.

Who are the people you want to take care of the most?

_____

_____

_____

_____

_____

_____

31

How Do You Make Your Body Feel Good?

"Exercise and Eat Healthy Every Single Day"

Not only do you need to brush your teeth every day, but you also need to move your body. By moving around, you push your blood to every part of your body, making you feel extremely good.

Eating well is even more important because that is the fuel you need to exercise.

What is your
favorite exercise?
What fruit
will you try today
or tomorrow?

33

Growing Up & Pursuing Your Dreams!

We've arrived at our fourth and final section: **Growing Up & Pursuing Your Dreams!** First, we'll discuss how being a great communicator is important. Next, we'll talk about how working hard and putting in the effort will improve your chances of success. Finally, we'll discuss how running your own business can be a great job.

What Do You Want to Be When You Grow Up?

"A Great Communicator"

Communication is
very important.

Being a great communicator
means that you can listen and
talk to any person about
any topic.

Great communication will
allow you to do anything you
want when you grow up.

What is one thing
that we can talk
about now?

_____

_____

_____

_____

_____

Do You Always Need to Work Hard?

"Always Work Hard To Make Your Own Luck"

The best combination is using your mind to work smart and dedicating yourself whole-heartedly to what you want to accomplish. There is no substitute for hard work.

People notice and respect hard workers. You will always do well if you put in the time and effort.

What do you work hard at?

What Do Good Businesses Have?

"Profits!"

Whether you're trying to make someone smile or laugh, or running a business, you want a good outcome.

In a business, that good outcome is called a profit. You get a profit when you get more back than you gave out.

Profits are like a reward for a job well done. And who doesn't love a prize after a good deed?

Did you make anyone laugh or smile today?

The
End

About The Authors

For the past 25 years **Mort Greenberg** has been a salesperson and sales manager for technology start-ups and larger media companies. Fighting his way up from an Account Executive to a role as a division President you can guess there were many challenges that needed to be overcome. Along the way Mort launched two companies, FitAd and MindFlight and learned many hard-fought lessons that start-ups are not always successful. He is a graduate of the State University of New York at New Paltz where he studied International Relations and Economics. While in college he started a company selling screen printing and promotional items to local businesses and on-campus organizations. At the same time, he also volunteered as a Congressional District Intern for the U.S. House of Representatives. He is an Eagle Scout and in junior high school bought several newspaper routes from neighborhood kids to create his first business. Mort is also the author of the *Revenue Vs. Sales*, a three book series that you can find on Amazon.com.

Carly Greenberg attends the University of Maryland's Smith School of Business with a double major in marketing and management. Carly's twin brother has autism, and she has helped him find his voice through her unique interactions with him. He is the original little guy with greatness. Carly is the original fearless girl, always helping others, volunteering, and finding ways to do more with less - all while having to put up with a crazy dad. Carly also holds a black belt in Tae Kwon Do.

www.ingramcontent.com/pod-product-compliance
Lightning Source LLC
Chambersburg PA
CBHW041555120626
46551CB00002B/217